# yukismart.com/b/654586

**baby**

**малюк**
*maliuk*

**boy**

**хлопчик**
*khlopchyk*

**friends**

**друзі**
*druzi*

**girl**

**дівчинка**
*divchynka*

**smile**

**посміхатися**
*posmikhatysia*

**cry**

**плакати**
*plakaty*

**hair**

**волосся**
*volossia*

**eye**

**око**
*oko*

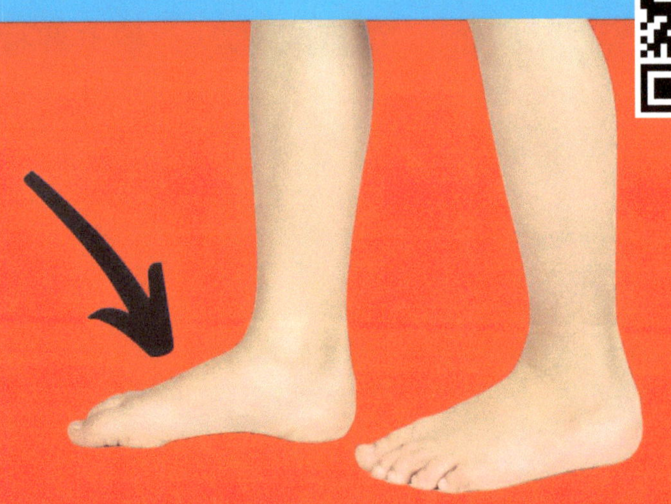

**foot**

**стопа**
*stopa*

**hand**

**кисть**
*kyst*

**nose**

ніс
*nis*

**teeth**

зуби
*zuby*

**ear**

вухо
*vukho*

**tongue**

язик
*iazyk*

**sun**

**сонце**
*sontse*

**moon**

**місяць**
*misiats*

**star**

**зірка**
*zirka*

# tree

**дерево**
*derevo*

# bird

**пташка**
*ptashka*

coat

**пальто**
*palto*

pants

**штани**
*shtany*

**dress**

**сукня**
*suknia*

**shoes**

**черевики**
*cherevyky*

## red

**червоний**

*chervonyi*

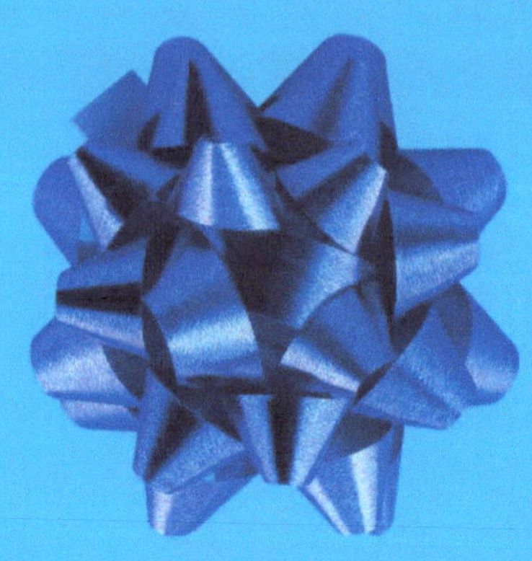

## blue

**синій**

*synii*

## yellow

**жовтий**

*zhovtyi*

## pink

**рожевий**

*rozhevyi*

**white**

**білий**
*bilyi*

**green**

**зелений**
*zelenyi*

**black**

**чорний**
*chornyi*

multicolored
різнокольоровий
riznokolorovyi

# rainbow

## веселка
*veselka*

**apple**

яблуко
*iabluko*

**banana**

банан
*banan*

**tomato**

помідор
*pomidor*

**orange**

апельсин
*apelsyn*

**carrot**

**морква**

*morkva*

**peas**

**горошинки**

*horoshynky*

**potato**

**картопля**

*kartoplia*

**corn**

**кукурудза**

*kukurudza*

**lemon**

**лимон**
*lymon*

**grapes**

**виноград**
*vynohrad*

**pear**

**груша**
*hrusha*

**watermelon**

**кавун**
*kavun*

# zucchini

**Кабачок-цукіні**
*Kabachok-tsukini*

# egg

**яйце**
*iaitse*

# mushroom

**гриб**
*hryb*

**square**

**квадрат**
*kvadrat*

**circle**

**коло**
*kolo*

# rectangle

**прямокутник**
*priamokutnyk*

# triangle

**трикутник**
*trykutnyk*

**cat**

кішка
*kishka*

**dog**

собака
*sobaka*

**fish**

**риба**
*ryba*

**cow**

**корова**
*korova*

**duck**

**качка**
*kachka*

**chick**

**курча**
*kurcha*

**hen**

**курка**
*kurka*

**frog**

**жаба**
*zhaba*

**pig**

**свиня**
*svynia*

**rabbit**

**кролик**
*krolyk*

**mouse**

**миша**
*mysha*

**horse**

**кінь**
*kin*

**sheep**

**вівця**
*vivtsia*

**flower**

**квітка**
*kvitka*

**butterfly**

**метелик**
*metelyk*

**ladybug**

**божа корівка**
*bozha korivka*

**snail**

**равлик**
*ravlyk*

# cake

## тістечко

*tistechko*

# bread

## хліб
*khlib*

**clock**

**годинник**
*hodynnyk*

**key**

**ключ**
*kliuch*

**book**

**книга**
*knyha*

**ball**

**м'яч**
*m'iach*

**table**

стіл
*stil*

**plate**

тарілка
*tarilka*

**chair**

стілець
*stilets*

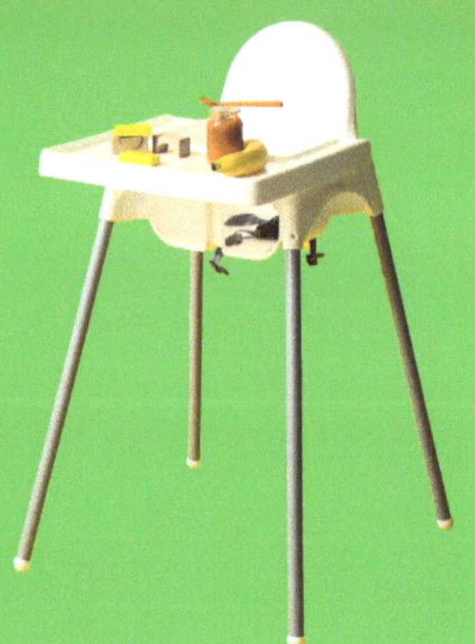

**high chair**

стільчик для годування
*stilchyk dlia hoduvannia*

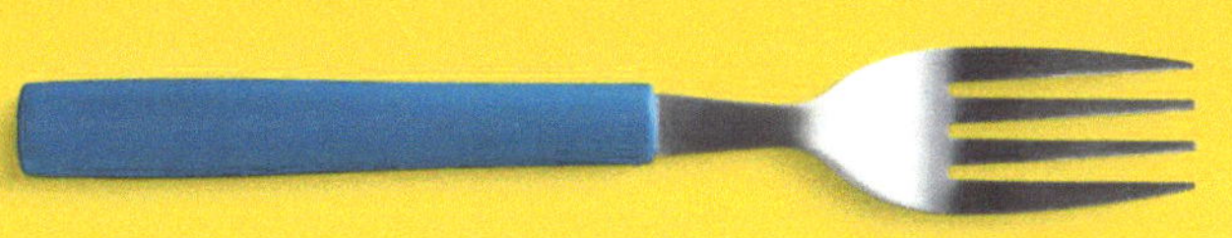

**fork**

**виделка**
*vydelka*

**knife**

**ніж**
*nizh*

**spoon**

**ложка**
*lozhka*

**cup**

**чашка**
*chashka*

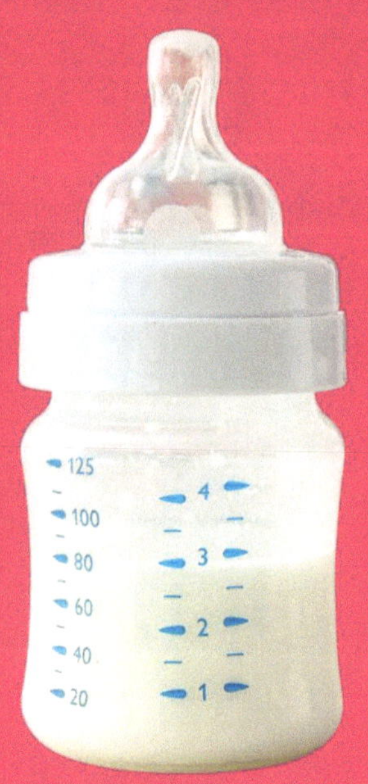

# baby bottle

## дитяча пляшечка
*dytiacha pliashechka*

# glass

## стакан
*stakan*

## bed

ліжко
*lizhko*

## crib

дитяче ліжко
*dytiache lizhko*

## teddy bear

плюшевий ведмедик
*pliushevyi vedmedyk*

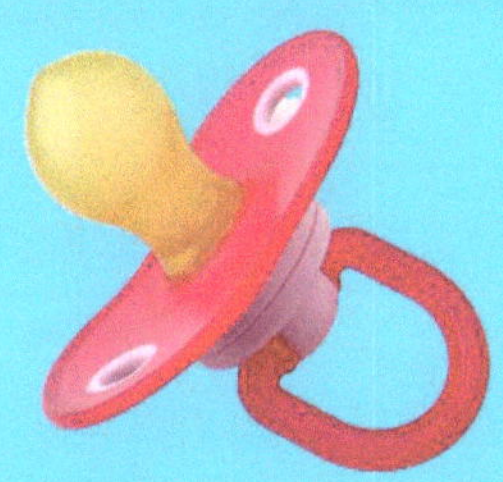

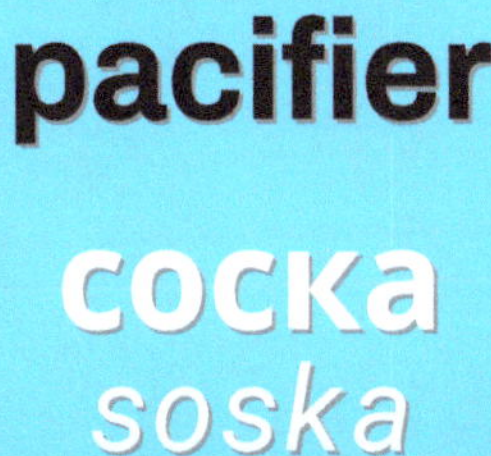

## pacifier

соска
*soska*

## towel

**рушник**
*rushnyk*

## sink

**раковина**
*rakovyna*

## toothbrush

**зубна щітка**
*zubna shchitka*

## soap

**мило**
*mylo*

**toilet**

**унітаз**
*unitaz*

**potty**

**дитячий горщик**

*dytiachyi horshchyk*

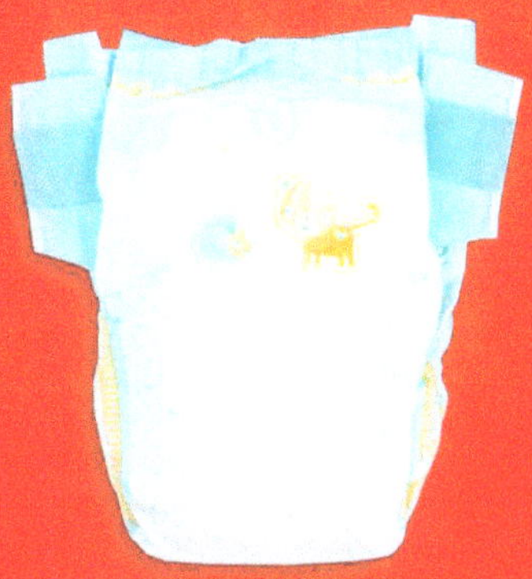

**diaper**

**підгузник**

*pidhuznyk*

**car**

**машина**
*mashyna*

**bike**

**велосипед**
*velosyped*

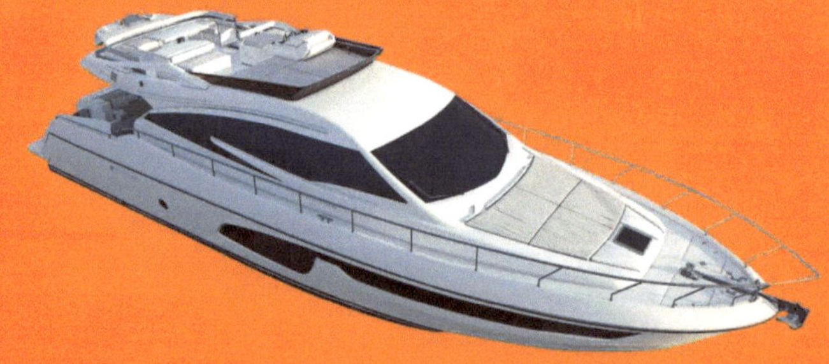

**plane**

**літак**
*litak*

**boat**

**човен**
*choven*

**firetruck**

**пожежна машина**
*pozhezhna mashyna*

**train**

**ПОТЯГ**
*potiah*

**toys**

## іграшки
*ihrashky*

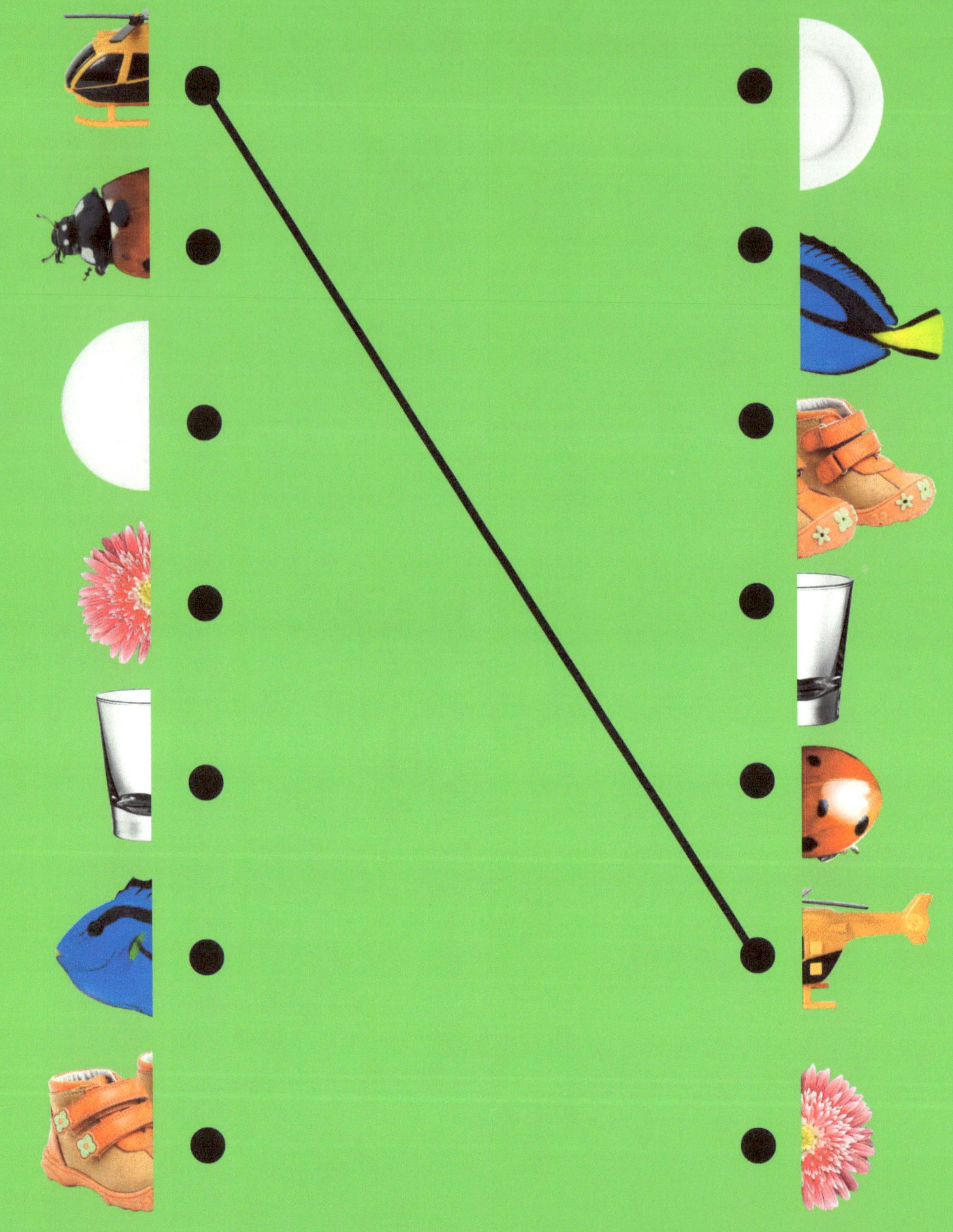

www.ingramcontent.com/pod-product-compliance
Lightning Source LLC
LaVergne TN
LVHW071636180726

843512LV00002B/325